Winni
Prayer War

Kjell Sjöberg

New Wine Press

New Wine Press
P. O. Box 17
Chichester
England PO20 6YB

Bible quotations are from the NIV New International Version. Copyright © 1973, 1978, International Bible Society, published by Hodder and Stoughton.

ISBN 0 947852 87 5

the Lord is my strength and my song! Ps. 118:14

Contents

About the author

Kjell Sjöberg was born in Stockholm, Sweden in 1933, the eldest son of six children. His father and grandfather were both Pentecostal ministers. It was at the age of 18 that he came into a first-hand experience of God through faith in Jesus Christ. Six months later he started to preach. At the age of 23 he planted his first church in Sweden. In 1961 he went to Pakistan with his wife Lena, and together they worked there for 11 years, planting churches and starting the Full Gospel Bible School in Lahore. After returning to Sweden in 1972, he started a church that in ten years grew to 650 members in Järfälla, a suburb of Stockholm.

For ten years he was a leader of Intercessors for Sweden. Since 1983 he has ministered in many countries on all the continents, teaching about prayer and spiritual warfare and working with prayer movements praying for cities and nations.

He has written a number of books, including *The*

Prophetic Church (1982), *Enthusiasm* (1984), and *Spiritual Vikings* (1985). During his brief periods at home he lives at Bro, near Stockholm, where he is able to share his family life with Lena and with their son, his wife and the five grandchildren who live nearby.

Chapter 1

Taking Responsibility

The church is responsible for its area

I remember sitting with a business man in Sweden as he read Ezekiel 22:30 to me, sharing with me his conviction that the Lord is searching for men to build up the wall and to stand in the gap on behalf of the nation. He pointed at me and said, "Kjell, are you that man?" I was the only person in the room with him, so I could not look to anyone else! So I said, "Yes, I am ready to take my responsibility to be an intercessor for my nation." I have carried that responsibility of being an intercessor for the past 15 years.

The Lord is searching for intercessors. He wants men everywhere to lift up holy hands in prayer (1 Tim. 2:8). For the last 15 years, I have worked among individuals and churches who are praying for their place, their area. The strongest support has come from intercessors who know their locality, and

7

define their calling as a responsibility for a specific geographical area.

When two or three meet together in prayer, they and the Lord Jesus together form a cabinet, an executive body of government making collective decisions in prayer.

We shall reign with Christ in the coming ages, but today we are in training by praying for our area. The Lord is calling you to be a member of the shadow cabinet of intercessors. Behind the scenes, together with Christ, you will influence what is going on in your city, town or locality. For this high purpose the Lord has called out his church from the world.

The word used in Greek to mean "church", *ecclesia*, was from the earliest times a word used to describe a council or group of citizens appointed and gathered together to determine the affairs of the town and locality. This group became the local authority, taking responsibility for its area. The church is an assembly chosen of God so that He can have his people in an area, who take the responsibility of "bringing in" God's kingdom by praying "Your kingdom come".

Sometimes we have divided up God's church into a series of sectarian groups, splitting up God's purpose of wholeness for the role of the church in the life of the community. It is only when we become free from sectarianism that we, together with all God's people, can take full responsibility for the place we live in.

Becoming rooted in the place where we live

God's intention for his ancient people was that they should be rooted in the Promised Land for ever. Each family had its allocated inheritance; the land was divided up into lots for them, even before they entered it. Each tribe knew its district, each family knew about its roots which were to be in a particular place. When the instruction came *"I will give you every place where you set your foot"*, everyone knew what place was referred to. Each had been given a place, even if it was still in enemy hands. In the same way, God wants you to have your roots in a place, and you in turn need to give yourself to that place. Even if you are not going to stay there all your life, you need to be willing to have a life-long commitment. You cannot convince others that you are ready to invest your life in a place, and at the same time be longing to get away from it. God can give you a strong love for the place where you live, and it is from a God-given love for a place that there grows a responsibility for the people living there.

God gives geographical areas of responsibility

The taking of responsibility for a geographical area was a principle also in the early days of the Church. Paul speaks of *"the field God has assigned to us"*, *"our area of activity"*, *"another man's territory"* (2 Cor. 10:13–16). He considered that God gave to individuals geographical areas of responsibility so that the gospel could be spread abroad and the Church established.

I believe in a ministry of intercession that is directed to places and to nations, and therefore, I am seeking those who have such a ministry for their particular areas. Each of them takes responsibility for his locality and keeps himself informed about what is going on in it. Some people are only in touch with what is happening in their own church. They do not know much about what is going in other churches, not about what is happening in their local council.

An intercessor who prays for his locality and keeps himself in touch with what is happening in the area, in time becomes extremely well-informed about it. His aim should be to know as much about the community as does the editor of the local paper or the senior police officer.

A good friend of mine, who was visiting a meeting in a town near his where I was preaching, came and whispered in my ear before he left the meeting, to tell me what had been going on in his town. He knew what I expected to hear, as I had just been visiting his town for a weekend of prayer gatherings, when we had prayed for the town. We had prayed for the town council, because the decision-making process had been frustrated by strong personal confrontations and open conflict between leaders. The town had been known for its resistance against receiving immigrants. Now, however, he told me of answers to our prayer. The atmosphere in the town council had changed for the better after we had prayed, and the council had decided after all to allow immigrants in. My friend was a lay preacher in his church. His account of events showed that since he had started to pray for his town, he had become well-informed and had grown to maturity in taking responsibility for his community.

Jesus talked with his disciples over a period of forty days about the kingdom of God, but it does not follow in practice that you can talk about the kingdom of God with all Christians. When can you? When you meet those who live and walk in the Spirit and take account of the invisible, those who have understood how important is the unity of the people of God and have taken responsibility for their locality – with such people you can talk about the kingdom of God.

The coming of Jesus and the future of the community

The Jews who were carried into captivity in Babylon were exposed to false prophets, who foretold that they would shortly be going back to their land. If they had listened to this false theology, they would never have become rooted in the place where they were living. The message of Jeremiah to them was that they should be prepared for a long stay in the place where they were, and that their future lay in praying for the welfare of their new city.

> *"Build houses and settle down; plant gardens and eat what they produce. Marry and have sons and daughters; find wives for your sons and give your daughters in marriage, so that they too may have sons and daughters. Increase in number*

> *there; do not decrease. Also, seek the peace and prosperity of the city to which I have carried you into exile. Pray to the Lord for it, because if it prospers, you too will prosper."*
>
> (Jer. 29:5–7)

The word of the prophet Jeremiah can apply also to ourselves, who live in the present evil age and look for redemption by the coming of Jesus. Christians can have a wrong view of the second coming of our Lord Jesus, which leads to a passive attitude of escape. The main purpose of the coming of Jesus is not to evacuate the Christians, but to establish the lordship of Christ over the earth. I believe in the rapture, when the bride of Christ will be caught up in the clouds to meet him in the air, but a subsequent event will be to follow Jesus back to earth and to the centre of events. Jesus is coming to the Mount of Olives, he is coming to Jerusalem, to one of the world's capital cities. When he comes to that city, Jerusalem will become an object of praise on the earth. The future of my own town also lies with the coming of the Lord. Then, my town will become a place filled with the glory of God. Now, for the time being we are working to prepare our town for the coming of the King. The knowledge of Jesus' coming spurs us on to take our responsibility for our area.

Seek peace and prosperity for your town

The Christians in any place should take responsibility for it by praying for it. The destiny of a church is bound up with the destiny of its community. When the population of a place grows and new possibilities for work are created, there are greater opportunities for the church to grow and to share in the general optimism for the future. If a place becomes depopulated with its factories closing down causing unemployment, the church can easily become affected by the depressed atmosphere. When God's people use the weapon of prayer, they are not trapped by rising or lowering trends, but take part in shaping the history of their local area.

The answers to prayer that we experience are a foretaste of the kingdom to come. These answers become a prophetic testimony, through which the Lord demonstrates on a small scale what he will do for the world on a large scale when Jesus returns.

Answer to prayer – a calm New Year

Over the New Year holiday 1986–87, all the churches in Oskarshamn, a seaport town on the Baltic coast of Sweden, arranged a united evangelistic campaign. During the week, about 400 Christians met every morning praying for the town. On New Year's Eve, the Christians met in the main square, in a temperature of minus 10 Celsius, to pray publicly. There was a worship team of two hundred young people. There was no preaching, but a well-known evangelist from the town interviewed the leader of the town council about the future of the town and its problems.

The interview gave us areas to cover in prayer. The council leader was not a believer, but he remained with us while we prayed about the problems of the town. One problem was the increase in the number of young people involved in alcohol and drug abuse. The Lord gave me faith to pray publicly for the town's campaign among young people against alcohol abuse, and I remember that while I was praying, I was holding the yellow pamphlet describing the campaign. I prayed that the community would succeed in this campaign, and that the people would give God the honour for his care of the town when the prayer was answered.

After the weekend, when the local newspaper reported about our public prayer meeting for the town, with pictures of all the praying Christians and the leader of the council, there also appeared a headline, "New Year celebrations the calmest for decades":–

> *This was the calmest New Year I have experienced during my 25 years or service. Jan-Erik Eneman, duty officer in charge of the Oskarshamn police during the holiday, was genuinely pleasantly surprised about his tour of duty. "We didn't need to arrest a single person for drunkenness during the night between New Year's Eve and New Year's Day. I believe it's the first time for decades that no arrest was needed."*
> *(Oskarshamn Times, 2 January 1987).*

When God's people take responsibility for their area, seek its welfare and pray for it, then we shall often read good news of answered prayer in the local newspapers.

We have a promise that when we pray for the authorities, we shall live peaceful and quiet lives. When we pray for the town, the Lord is victorious over the evil, destructive powers. God's peace settles on the town, so that we are able to preach and evangelise without being hindered or disturbed by anything. A revival does not go deep unless it also has an effect on the life of the neighbourhood.

Chapter 2

Being Conquerors

We are called to conquer towns and places for Jesus Christ. We are born to be conquerors. The promise was given to Abraham:

> *"I will surely bless you and make your descend-ants as numerous as the stars in the sky and as the sand on the seashore. Your descendants will take possession of the cities of their enemies."*
>
> (Gen. 22:17)

Born to be conquerors

God works with a long-range plan to conquer the earth. He promised Abraham descendants who would be born to become conquerors. The same promise was given to Rebekah when she left her own family to marry Isaac.

> *"And they blessed Rebekah and said to her, 'Our*

17

sister, may you increase to thousands upon thousands; may your offspring possess the gates of their enemies.' "

(Gen. 24:60).

The promise of Rebekah was that she would bear children who would become conquerors. We are born to be conquerors.

"For everyone born of God has overcome the world. This is the victory that has overcome the world, even our faith."

(1 John 5:4).

We are among the children promised to Abraham. Therefore, we can accept personally that which is promised for us. Abraham received the promise that he would inherit the world; the promise would be fulfilled through his descendants. You will share in it too and possess the gates of your enemies. Gates are the entrances to towns and other places, and he who prays must knock on the gates. Now is the time for you to knock on the closed gates of the town so that they will be opened to you and to God's people. In modern times we no longer depend on gates that open and shut in order to get into our towns. But there are other gates today, that we have to go through in order to get into a place. The gates are the key persons, the decision-makers, they are groups such as chambers of commerce, political groups, orders, clubs, large businesses. They are not our enemies. But we believe also that there are demonic principalities ruling over towns and places. They try to make use of key persons in the town, and these in turn become the closed gates of the town that hinder the representatives of the Kingdom of God from coming in and gaining influence for God's kingdom.

Jesus says of his Church that the gates of hell will not overcome it (Matt. 16:18). In the gates of hell, councils are held to enable the principalities and powers to gain control of the power bases built up in places and centres of population, and so maintain their control in the world. The object of the power bases is to be able to resist invasion by the kingdom of heaven, initiated by Jesus Christ and continued by the church and by the hosts of angels supporting it. Our role is to be the invasion force that goes into the attack against the stronghold of hell.

> *"The Lord Almighty . . . will be a spirit of justice to him who sits in judgment, a source of strength to those who turn back the battle at the gate."*

> (Is. 28:5–6)

Born to reach greater heights

We are born to be conquerors. That means a change of attitude in order to become conquerors in practice.

Christians in Sweden have not been conquerors in recent decades. We have retreated. Many churches have decreased in numbers. We have given up positions that we once held. We have fallen into the habit of being a minority that has to yield to the claims of other groups. We have been willing to compromise positions that our forefathers fought for. We have given up ethical standards and have accepted, for example, legalised abortion. We have ceased holding morning prayers at the start of the school day. Also, we used to follow the custom that on the last day of the school year, before the summer holidays, the whole school sang a well-known psalm, "The season of flowers is upon us"; that custom has been abolished. The time in school for Christian instruction has given way to the teaching of comparative religions. In fact, we have been a majority who have allowed ourselves to be frightened by a small, loud-mouthed minority into making these concessions. In our legislation we have yielded up the primacy of the marriage relationship to other forms of living together, opening the way to acceptance of unmarried and homosexual couples living together.

All the concessions in our Swedish legislation were carried out in co-operation with Christian leaders. The history of those concessions is written in memoranda sent by official church bodies to our Government. If we are to be an overcoming Christian people again, we must repent of this attitude of concession which characterises the majority of Swedish Christians, and break free from it.

My brother Stanley, who is also a Christian pastor, used an illustration from Harvard University, where someone was carrying out research into the behaviour of fleas. They put some fleas into a glass cube. In the lid of the cube were ping-pong balls. When the fleas jumped upwards they hit their heads on the ping-pong balls. Then they lowered the balls to a height of ten centimetres. The fleas, who could jump much higher, hit their heads on the balls. So they took to jumping only to a height of eight centimetres. After that, the lid of the cube was removed and the walls lowered to ten centimetres, and none of the fleas jumped out. They had become conditioned to an artificial limiting of their powers. In the same way, we are born to conquer and to reach greater heights. But we have been affected by all the times we have hit our heads on the roof and failed. Our failure, both as individuals and as churches, does not represent the true extent of our God-given power and calling. We have conditioned ourselves to the satanic resistance, which Satan keeps up so that he can maintain his hold over places and prevent the conquerors from capturing them.

Others who think in terms of conquering

When the homosexuals held a propaganda week in Stockholm, they gathered for a meeting to discuss strategy. We had a spy among them who reported on their discussions. After holding a number of these propaganda weeks in Stockholm and making their voices heard in the major cities of our country, they decided it was the time to conquer smaller places for their message and life-style. They discussed the setting-up of a model project in some small community in Sweden to show by example how the homosexual life-style had become accepted. They would go into the schools to witness about their homosexual or lesbian life-style. They would establish their presence in smaller communities. Their people sought jobs as theatre managers and started popular disco-clubs to attract young people. These people believe they have a message, and they want to conquer places for their message.

The Satanists are also out to conquer Sweden. In one group in Stockholm, they set aside seven people with important assignments to spread their influence in Sweden. They pray for chaos and bloodshed, anarchy and terrorism. They seek key positions for their members from which they can exercise their influence, and have already found such positions in finance, as politicians, as authors of children's books, as athletics trainers, and as psychiatrists. They are building a network of contacts in the Scandinavian capitals, a network with many international ramifications.

The anthroposophists in the town of Järna, who are concerned with religious syncretism based on theosophy and practising plant meditation, animal meditation and earth meditation, are trying to take over the town for their message. In Järna they have forty or so enterprises such as their own schools, hospital, bank, mill, shops and collective farms. They are establishing a spiritually based community to be a model for Swedish society as a whole.

At a meeting held by the occult sect Summit Lighthouse in Malmö, it was taught that a person can, through meditation, set up such an aura of radiation round himself that he can influence the thinking of an entire city. These people are aiming to change the thinking of the whole population by meditation.

What I want to show is that it is no longer only a military term to talk of conquering. The occult movements are keen to conquer places for the kingdom of the Antichrist. Since so many other, unclean powers and ideas are out to conquer places, we Christians must free ourselves from all passivity and attitude of defeat, and rouse ourselves to carry out that which God has called us to do.

Equipment for conquering

> *"A wise man attacks the city of the mighty and pulls down the stronghold in which they trust."*
> (Prov. 21:22)

God can use a single man to take a city, and God can give the wisdom needed for such a mission. If we lack wisdom, we are to ask God for it. If you lack the wisdom to take a city for Jesus, you are to ask God for it. It is true that a condition of conquering a place for the kingdom of God is unity among God's people. But God wants to use individuals who are taking the responsibility for unity among his church, to take the initiative in capturing the city for Christ.

> *"Like a city whose walls are broken down is a man who lacks self-control."*
> (Prov. 25:28)

23

When God takes charge of a person and starts to govern his mind and thoughts, it is worth as much as the conquest of a whole city. God wants to establish his order in a community, but the first stage in the establishing of his order is the bringing of his order into one man's mind and thoughts. He does not want to commit the resources of Heaven to a conquest that leads to chaos. The first step in conquering a place is that the rebellious mind of one individual is laid at the feet of Jesus and that the lordship of Christ is proclaimed over that mind, so that that person begins to think and act in accordance with God's thoughts, instead of acting in accordance with man's thoughts.

He saved the city, but who remembered him afterwards?

> *"There was once a small city with only a few people in it. And a powerful king came against it, surrounded it and built huge siegeworks against it. Now there lived in that city a man poor but wise, and he saved that city by his wisdom. But nobody remembered that poor man."*
>
> (Eccl. 9:14–15)

What God wants to do is so great and revolutionary. When the kingdom of God comes with power, it means deliverance for places and nations. But we can only work together with God in the great works he wants to do, if we are humble. It is the meek who will inherit the earth. If we are seeking honour for our own name, we are hindering God's plans for the end time. Conquest takes place in the unseen, on the spiritual level. Afterwards it manifests itself visibly. That is the way conquering prayer works. As long as we operate on that level, there will be no one who can take outward honour for himself. We can get no greater satisfaction than that of having been obedient and having carried out Jesus' commands. He who prays can identify himself with the man who saved the city but was forgotten after deliverance came. God must be given all the glory. Jesus Christ must be exalted and welcomed.

Chapter 3

Every place where you set your foot

"I will give you every place where you set your foot, as I promised Moses."

(Joshua 1:3)

God has already given it, so we go frankly and fearlessly to take possession of it. We have the Lord's deed of conveyance in our hand, and so we can go and evict the unlawful occupiers from the house.

"The Lord your God brings you into the land . . . to give you – a land with large, flourishing cities you did not build."

(Deut. 6:10)

"Then the Lord will drive out all these nations before you, and you will dispossess nations larger and stronger than you. Every place where you set your foot will be yours."

(Deut. 11:23–24)

This promise is given to a minority of conquerors and it has inspired many Christians to go on prayer walks, prayer journeys and praise marches. We set out feet down in a place in order to possess territory for the kingdom, when we are breaking new ground among unreached people, or going into areas closed to the gospel, or coming as the first Christians into an area. We challenge the places occupied by the powers of darkness, relying on Jesus' authority, given to us,

> *"to trample on snakes and scorpions and to over-come all the power of the enemy"*
>
> (Luke 10:19).

The feet of the conquerors are identified with the feet of Jesus. This was also said of the Christians in Rome and the victory they were going to win in their city:

> *"The God of peace will soon crush Satan under your feet."*
>
> (Rom. 16:20)

Places can be full of evil

> *"Fallen! Fallen is Babylon the Great! She has become a home for demons and a haunt for every evil spirit, a haunt for every unclean and detestable bird."*
>
> (Rev. 18:2)

28

When you walk around in the city of Rome, you can see large, unclean birds, eagles, both on old buildings and also on new Government buildings. What kind of art is this, adorning buildings, parks and squares? Frequently the figures have shamanistic features or are derived from stories of the Greek gods or other pagan sources. The Bible takes for granted that certain places can be filled with darkness, full of evil spirits, a haunt for all evil. Babylon, as a gathering place for all evil spirits, speaks to us of a polarisation in the last days. Where do the evil spirits go to, when they are driven out? – They look for other evil spirits. Certain parts of the Earth have become so attractive to the evil spirits that they act as rubbish tips, dumping grounds where expelled spirits gather. There are places where prayers are ineffective, because Christians persist in splitting and living in disunity. Is your locality going to be a rubbish tip for evil spirits, or a liberated area?

Places where the Lord lives

> *"And the name of the city from that time on will be: THE LORD IS THERE."*
>
> (Ezek. 48:35)

God's people, and those who pray, have the keys to a place. If they become slack in intercession, they are like a farmer ceasing to plough and cultivate his field. The evil spirits, like weeds, are free to grow again and to regain the upper hand. But if God's people maintain their position of victory and take the responsibility for intercession in their area, then they become channels for God's fullness, so that all can testify: Here the Lord truly lives amongst his people.

Something that must be put in order before Jesus comes

We have a commission in every place to make ready for the coming of Jesus.

> *"Who can endure the day of his coming?"*
> (Mal. 3:2)

If the Elijah ministry has not been done, if no preparation has been made, places and nations will be condemned to utter destruction. (Mal. 4:6) That day when Jesus assembles his bride in the skies, at his coming, will be a day of judgment for the world. What we call the tribulation and the wrath of God will be like a spring-cleaning, before Jesus comes to reign in peace on the earth. Until that happens, we have the opportunity of cleaning up the house, getting rid of everything that can cause the wrath of the Lamb, so as to save the place from the judgment of God.

> *"I tell you the truth, you will not finish going through the cities of Israel before the Son of Man comes."*
> (Matt. 10:23)

We used this word from the Bible as our theme text

when we travelled round 21 places in Israel on a prayer journey and visited messianic congregations, house churches and prayer groups. In one town I met an old intercessor, who was also a watchman. He had lived a long time in the town and had studied its history. He was able to point out the "high places" where occult sacrifices were made in ancient times and where the Asherah poles had stood. He knew where the modern occult movements met, and which house was a centre for drug traffic. He had assembled all this knowledge in order to contribute to putting the town in order for the coming of the Lord. We became aware that the time was not ripe to deal with this on the day we visited the town. There was no unity, or capacity to bear common burdens, among the believers in the town. We left behind us something uncompleted, but the disunity had to be put right before the coming of Jesus if the place was to be spared from the wrath of the Lamb.

This does not only apply to the towns of Israel; it concerns the capital cities of the world as well. The unfinished work exists in the towns of Sweden. It applies to your own town. What are the things in the place where you live that must be put in order before Jesus comes?

As many idols as there are towns

"You have as many gods as you have towns, O Judah; and the altars you have set up to burn incense to that shameful god Baal are as many as the streets of Jerusalem."

(Jer. 11:13)

Behind every idol demanding to be worshipped, there stood a demonic power seeking to control the town. Satan has a strategy to enable him to maintain his reign over earth, and this is to have his demonic princes disposed in such a way as to have power over every concentration of population on earth. Wherever men have founded towns, Satan has sought to be in with them from the start.

Some towns were founded with violence and bloodshed.

> *"Woe to him who builds a city with bloodshed and establishes a town by crime!"*
>
> (Hab. 2:12)

When we pray for a town, we need to ask: How was its foundation laid? Was there anything in connection with its founding that gave Satan an invitation? Sometimes, towns were built around a place of sacrifice, or a temple of a false god, as their centre. The Romans founded towns in the name of their god Jupiter.

Satan has also looked for points of attachment with the leaders of cities. In Egypt and Babylonia and in other heathen cultures, the one who became leader has a working relationship with the local gods. Pharaoh was an incarnation of the sun-god Amun. Often the king of a city was at the same time the high priest of the demonic power controlling it.

When Joshua was writing the history of how the Promised Land was taken, he counted all the kings he had defeated.

"These are the kings of the land whom the Israeli-tes had defeated and whose territory they took over east of the Jordan . . ."

(Jos. 12:1)

"the king of Jericho	*one*
the king of Ai (near Bethel)	*one*
the king of Jerusalem	*one*
the king of Hebron	*one*

. . .

thirty-one kings in all."

(Jos. 12:9, 10, 24).

One king for each town. These kings were men, of course, but they were high priests also, each a priest for the idol controlling the city he ruled over. They were kings and therefore they were in communi-cation with the ruling principality over the town.

Translated into our situation and transferred on the spiritual level to the power structures in the spirit world: the king of Stockholm, one; the king of London, one; the king of New York, one. There are as many demonic princes as there are towns and places in our countries.

The power structure in Tyre consisted of both a demonic prince and an earthly king and there was a definite link between them. Satan has as much power on earth as men provide room for him. He wants to be worshipped, and to those who worship him, he gives power over towns and nations. There are always people seeking power for themselves on these conditions. (Ezek. 28)

If we are going to capture a place for the Lord, we must bind the strong man, and then we can plunder his goods. Through prayer war we disarm and expose the evil powers. We frustrate their plans. We proclaim over them the victory which Jesus has already won on the Cross, where he disarmed the powers and authorities of the spirit world.

Expose the strongholds of darkness

We must also gain understanding about where the strong man in a place has his strongholds or points of attachment. Ezekiel in a vision saw twenty-five men at the entrance to the temple of the Lord.

> *"The Lord said to me, 'Son of man, these are the men who are plotting evil and giving wicked advice in this city.' "*
> (Ezek. 11:1–3; see also 8:7–11, 16)

When we take up a floor covering, such as cork tiling or carpeting that has been glued down, we discover that in some places it comes away easily, but in others it sticks fast and has to be scraped off. Our task in prayer is to roll away the covering of darkness that exists over a place. It is like a sticky mass. When we start lifting it off to make room for the glory of God, it becomes clear where its points of attachment are. Then we have to go in and prise it loose with our prayer weapons. The powers of darkness can only remain in a place where they have people, occult societies, secret orders, unconfessed sins, curses and blood-guilt, that give them entrance and points of attachment.

The light that rises over a place

The cloak of darkness that covers the earth will soon be rolled up and its place will be taken by the light of God's glory. This is stated to a town:

> *"Arise, shine, for your light has come,*
> *and the glory of the Lord rises upon you.*
> *See, darkness covers the earth*
> *and thick darkness is over the peoples,*
> *but the Lord rises upon you*
> *and his glory appears over you."*
>
> (Is. 60:1–2)

> *"For Zion's sake I will not keep silent,*
> *for Jerusalem's sake I will not remain quiet,*
> *till her righteousness shines out like the dawn,*
> *her salvation like a blazing torch."*
>
> (Is. 62:1)

What are we aiming for when we speak of conquering a place for Jesus Christ? We want to see the glory of the Lord fill the place, to see God's will done, and to experience as much as possible of the reign of Christ. This does not mean political influence. We pray for the political leaders. When the saints are reigning with Christ in prayer, they influence the spiritual atmosphere in a place and bring down into it the atmosphere of heaven. They are doing something that politicians cannot do.

When the powers of darkness are rolled away and thrown down (Rev. 12:9) prayer becomes easier, and it is easier to win people for God, and to live a godly life. The Holy Spirit is poured out on all men and the place becomes a liberated area. It is never complete until after the coming of Jesus, but we can, here and now, experience a foretaste of the kingdom that is to come.

The moth-eaten cloak that rolls away

I want you to understand your calling from God for your area, to prepare for its liberation and to ensure that what still remains to be done can be carried out before the Son of man comes. Therefore, I want to show you some scriptures that illuminate your task. There are passages that you have probably read passively without understanding your personal share in the process. The spiritual powers of evil rule in this dark world and in the heavenly regions. Through their rule, there is a layer of darkness that envelops the earth. In the course of time, this ancient cloak of curse has become like a moth-eaten cloak, full of holes. The light shines through. It is only a matter of time before this cloak of darkness rolls away altogether.

> *"Lift up your eyes to the heavens, look at the earth beneath; the heavens will vanish like smoke, the earth will wear out like a garment."*
> *"For the moth will eat them up like a garment;*

the worm will devour them like wool. But my righteousness will last for ever."

(Is. 51:6, 8)

See also Ps. 102:26–27; 2 Pet. 3:10–13; Matt. 24:29; Rom. 8:20–21; Rev. 6:14. These promises will be fulfilled at the coming of Jesus. We are taking part in the preparation. The process of liberation is carried out in co-operation with the intercessors, and those who are willing to capture their areas for Christ.

When Jacob came to Bethel, he came to a place on earth where the gate into the heavenly world stood open, and the angels could travel up and down. Jacob said,

> *"How awesome is this place! This is none other than the house of God; this is the gate of heaven."*

(Gen. 28:17)

In his dream he had seen a ladder resting on the earth, with its top reaching to heaven, and the angels of God ascending and descending on it. It was there that Jacob received the promise that he would be given the land as his inheritance. John's gospel expands on this open gate to heaven over Bethel:

> *"I tell you the truth, you shall see heaven open, and the angels of God ascending and descending on the Son of Man."*

(John 1:51)

37

Over Jesus, the heaven was open and the angels went freely up and down. The layer of darkness around the earth was broken through at the place where Jesus was, just as it was broken through at Bethel. The worn-out cloak of darkness, which will later be unwrapped and removed, is already worn and full of holes because of the coming and going of all the angels. We are involved in wearing out this covering, till it begins to look like a worn-out trouser-seat that shows the light through when you hold it up. In the first chapter of Hebrews, angels are mentioned several times in context with the author's quotation of Ps. 102:26–27.

> " '*In the beginning, O Lord, you laid the foundations of the earth, and the heavens are the work of your hands. They will perish, but you remain; they will all wear out like a garment. You will roll them up like a robe; like a garment they will be changed. But you remain the same, and your years will never end.' To which of the angels did God ever say, 'Sit at my right hand until I make your enemies a footstool for your feet'? Are not all angels ministering spirits sent to serve those who will inherit salvation?*"
>
> (Heb. 1:10–14)

When we pray and are in touch with the throne of God, angels are sent out. They travel up and down on their tasks, heaven's gate stands open, and each opening becomes a hole in the covering of darkness round the earth. Finally, the layer of darkness becomes so worn and full of holes that the time comes for it to be rolled away. Then the glory of God breaks through over the earth, and the Sun of righteousness rises, as on a cloudless morning. The darkness is then no longer there to prevent mankind from living in the light of God. It is this process that I take part in when I pray for my town, when I join in capturing it for Christ.

A growing work-load but no additional work-force

Satan's great problem is that from the beginning of his rebellion, the number of his spiritual forces, principalities and powers has remained constant, and these have to hold his kingdom together in the face of an increasing world population. Therefore, Satan has to find ways of controlling more and more men and women with his existing forces. One of his strategies has been to post his subordinates where there are cities and concentrations of people.

Another of his strategies has been to oppose, by any means, the increase of population. Therefore, it is part of his strategy that millions of human lives are snuffed out through abortions. Further, war and famine and disasters are all welcome events for the kingdom of darkness, as they hold down the world's population.

Satan tries to get people concentrated together, so that he can handle them more easily. He cannot do any new recruitment in the spirit world, and therefore he becomes increasingly desperate to capture people who are willing to dedicate themselves to his service. So it is his strategy to get men to enter into covenants with false gods. In occult movements and secret societies, there are always covenants or initiations for becoming a member. In this way, people become bound to one another through occult spiritual forces. The New Age movement works through a network. The powers of darkness need channels in the mass media through which they can control people in this world. Holding together this extensive network requires much fear to be generated among men and women. As long as Satan can hold people in fear, he can control large numbers of people with the use of only a small number of prison-warders and desperados. This is how we should view the power-structure of the kingdom of darkness.

The Antichrist is going to make a desperate attempt to keep the world's population under his control by demanding an initiation and a declaration of loyalty from those who serve him.

Satan has stretched his resources to the uttermost. Therefore, his kingdom becomes more and more vulnerable as the number of mature Christians grows larger, people who know how to use spiritual weapons. We are approaching the point where Satan's whole network will collapse. The book of Revelation describes the kingdom of the Antichrist as something that will collapse in chaos.

"Fallen! Fallen is Babylon the Great!"

(Rev. 18:2)

More light to expose the enemy's strategy

We must look more closely at the darkness and the old, tattered garment of curse that covers the earth. We need some light on what points of attachment it has in our own locality. These places can be the ancient pagan places of sacrifice, or high places. They can also include the strongholds of the kingdom of darkness in the mass media.

There are people who consciously co-operate with the forces of evil. These call the spirit power their master, their spirit guide or medium. Certain particular places, too, are dedicated to Satan. For instance, there are places where a satanic bible has been built into the foundation of a building, to show, right from its foundation, who the house belongs to. Again, sometimes in the past when a town was founded, children were sacrificed when the walls and gates were built. Innocent blood that has been shed, massacres and unsettled disputes or feuds, sins that have never been dealt with, are all points of attachment for the dark covering.

The spirits are tied to geographical territory: to mountains, islands, rivers and so on. People who worship demonic powers seek these spiritual power places, and worship stones, trees, watercourses, animals, and pursue meditation with the earth, plants or animals as do, for example, the anthroposophists. They bind themselves together with that part of the creation that is under God's judgment and is going to be rolled away. On the other hand, those who sing praises to God as creator who made the rivers, joining in the song of praise to the creator who is to be found in the whole of his creation, bind themselves with that part of the creation that is going to be freed and cleansed and will live on in God's glory in the kingdom of peace. The demonic powers have manipulated people into locating centres of population in the exact places where the demonic powers have their strongholds. The Holy Spirit will enable us to see the connection, and to expose the enemy's strategy, the way in which he has succeeded up to now in holding together his worn-out cloak of darkness around the earth.

Studying the history of a place to find the connections

If you really want to conquer your area for Jesus, and to clean it up and cut loose the points of contact with the covering of darkness, you will need people who can study local history to obtain material for the intercessors. You cannot take it for granted that Christians have always existed in your area with a proper understanding of outright prayer war, or an ability to get rid of what remains from pagan times. We know that there have been leaders who sold their cities to Satan in order to gain power over the population. For example, the Christians in one city in a Catholic country found historical documents showing that an earlier leader had dedicated the city to an image, the Black Madonna, and they realised that such an agreement needed to be broken. In a town that grew up beside a river, where the early inhabitants had worshipped the river and sacrificed human beings to the river-god by drowning, the Christians realised that they had to get rid of such an ancient pagan point of contact in order for the town to be freed and brought into the kingdom of light under Christ.

In Paris in former times the people worshipped the River Seine. Recently there was a state visit from India, and the Head of State brought some water from the holy river Ganges, worshipped in India. This holy water was poured out into the Seine in the course of an official ceremony. Actions such as this can re-activate the ancient pagan power-places back into life.

The strong man who has ruled an area for a long time will also have left an imprint on the history of that area. When we define the strong man, we want to have confirmation both from Scripture and from the history of the town. So, when you are researching the local history, look for the sins that have dominated the place. Look for blood-guilt; find out what pagan gods were worshipped, what minorities were oppressed – in particular, persecution or pogroms against the Jews. We study history, including church history, to discover the roots and points of linkage that have provided a legal right for demonic powers to occupy.

When researching, do not forget the positive aspect. Sometimes we have been given information about what God has spoken through prophecies and visions in the past. Through them, we have been able to discern God's prophetic calling for the city, and how he is planning to use the city as a blessing for the rest of the nation. By prayer, we are prepared to uproot every evil influence, and to strengthen everything planted by the Lord.

Chapter 4

Clearing the Ground

Sometimes in our intercessory prayer groups, when praying for one another and for places, we have spoken of clearing the ground, or carrying out a spiritual mopping-up operation. Where did this expression came from?

> *"You brought a vine out of Egypt; you drove out the nations and planted it. You cleared the ground for it, and it took root and filled the land."*

(Ps. 80:8–9)

In this way the Lord cleared the ground when he drove out the nations from the Promised Land, so that the people of God could take root and fill it. He did this by means of a strategy of helping one another. Those who had already occupied their allotted area were told to come and help their brothers. Aaron and Hur held up Moses' hands while Moses, in intercession, supported Joshua who was on the battlefield. (Ex. 17:9–16) The strategy was not to leave anyone alone on the battlefield. The best fighting morale is found in a unit where men know that if they are wounded, they will not be abandoned. The army of modern Israel is known for its promptness in taking care of the wounded, and this gives courage to its soldiers. Joshua began the conquest of the Promised Land by telling the Reubenites, the Gadites and the half-tribe of Manasseh to come over and fight for their brothers until the Lord gave them rest in the land (Jos. 1:12–15). This gives some indication of the purpose of the spiritual capturing of a place. Your locality should not be a place where you are hemmed in on every side by opposing forces, but a place that has been spiritually cleared so that God's people have room for action.

> *"The Lord gave them rest on every side, just as he had sworn to their forefathers. Not one of their enemies withstood them; the Lord handed all their enemies over to them. Not one of all the Lord's good promises to the house of Israel failed; every one was fulfilled."*

(Joshua 21:44–45)

When the goal had been achieved, Joshua could send home those who had stood at their brothers' side:

> *"For a long time now – to this very day – you have not deserted your brothers but have carried out the mission the Lord your God gave you. Now that the Lord your God has given your*

brothers rest as he promised, return to your homes.''

(Joshua 22:3–4)

It is never intended that anyone should take a city alone. Such a task is given to a people working together in unity, helping and supporting and encouraging one another, and so given over to one another that no one is ever left alone on the battle-field. Paul asks for support in prayer in his service for God so that he is not left in battle alone.

"I urge you, brothers, by our Lord Jesus Christ and by the love of the Spirit, to join me in my struggle by praying to God for me. Pray that I may be rescued from the unbelievers in Judea and that my service in Jerusalem may be accept-able to the saints there.''

(Rom. 15:30–31)

Paul needed help in the work of clearing up, to enable him to move ahead in his calling and to make way for his service.

Joshua warned the people of Israel not to inter-marry with idol-worshippers. If they did so, they would find themselves oppressed on every side.

"Then you may be sure that the Lord your God will no longer drive out these nations before you. Instead, they will become snares and traps for you, whips on your backs and thorns in your eyes, until you perish from this good land, which the Lord your God has given you.''

(Joshua 23:13)

There are many scriptures that show how the Lord made room for his servants and his people.

> *"You broaden the path beneath me, so that my ankles do not turn over."*
>
> (Ps. 18:36)

The enemy is concerned to get God's people confined and limited, to push them into a corner, to paralyse them. Interceding for a place is very like praying for those who hold spiritual offices. We pray that they may have rest on all sides, so that they can have room to exercise their calling. Clearing up a place is breaking up the ground, clearing it of stubble and stones. Even if it has in the past been stony ground or thorns, it can become good soil that bears fruit a hundred-fold. We have the confidence of faith that we can alter the spiritual situation. In the name of Jesus, we can drive out the powers that seek to confine God's people. We can clear away former sins that have caused a place to be cursed, and we can clear away past actions of the flesh, things done that God never asked for.

> *"Every plant that my heavenly Father has not planted will be pulled up by the roots"*
> said Jesus. (Matt. 15:13). That is what clearing-up is.

> *"But Joshua said to the house of Joseph – to Ephraim and Manasseh – 'You are numerous and very powerful. You will have not only one*

48

allotment but the forested hill country as well.
Clear it, and its farthest limits will be yours;
though the Canaanites have iron chariots and
though they are strong, you can drive them
out.' "

(Joshua 17:17–18)

These scriptures have given us confidence to pray
for one another and for one another's localities. We
have invited Christian friends to "clearing-up days",
as in the following example.

An invitation to a clearing-up

"We want to invite you to a weekend of clearing-up
in Bro (the town where we live). We need help in
prayer to capture Bro for Christ. We have already
held previous clearing-up days, when we came
together in prayer and warfare in order to help by
clearing space for one another's work and for the
church of God in our area. These clearing-up days
have been characterised by a very warm comradeship
as we have battled together in the Holy Spirit. We
have compared ourselves to the Berserks (wild warriors of the Viking age, who fought on the battlefield
with a frenzied fury known as the 'berserker rage')
who were sent first into the battle to put fear into
the enemy. But during these clearing-up days we
have enjoyed fellowship full of joy, humour and
boyish high spirits.

"We need your help in this intercession and spiritual warfare, which is required if we are going to

take our town for Christ. When Joshua was seeking to occupy the Promised Land, he turned to the Reubenites, the Gadites and the half tribe of Manasseh and asked for their help: *'All your fighting men, fully armed, must cross over ahead of your brothers. You are to help your brothers until the Lord gives them rest, as he has done for you, and until they too have taken possession of the land that the Lord your God is giving them'.*

(Joshua 1:14–15)

"It is our experience that the Lord is leading us into more intensive intercession for places, so that they can be taken for Christ's kingdom and so that the spirit powers' grasp of them and the power structure over them may be crushed. We are coming together with a longing to learn more of this strategy, which we need in order to break the spirit world's hold over a place. Bro is built round the site of an ancient pagan cult, where the fertility-goddess Hern was worshipped. We shall be meeting in the school building, built on the actual site itself. In the name of Jesus, Bro will be cleansed from the ancient pagan cult, the modern occult movements and all other points of connection that remain from the regime of darkness. It is thrilling to be with Jesus!"

I have given this example to show how we obtained help for our local clearing-up days. If you want to take your city for Jesus, you need to take the initiative in clearing up. Before we can begin to build up or plant, we have to uproot, tear down, destroy and overthrow. (Jer. 1:10)

Chapter 5

Strategy for Conquering a City

Never start prayer warfare without having first received a strategy from the Lord. There are general principles of strategy that apply in any situation – the ABC of prayer war. But the Lord also has a unique strategy that applies in the particular situation, and he wants to reveal this to you so as to prepare you for the forthcoming battle. Joshua met the Lord's angel, who gave him detailed instructions on the strategy he was to use in capturing Jericho. Strategy is also revealed to us through our own knowledge if we have learnt to know the Lord's ways, and have read about the Lord's generals and the plans they used in achieving their victories. We need to know the Lord's priorities, to understand what is of first importance and what is secondary. Then, we need to make our plans with the help of sound advisers, those who are officers in the Lord's army. If we do not follow the proper order, our prayer meetings can end in chaos and confusion.

"Make plans by seeking advice; if you wage war, obtain guidance."

(Prov. 20:18)

"A wise man has great power, and a man of knowledge increases strength; for waging war you need guidance, and for victory many advisers."

(Prov. 24:5–6)

During our journeying round the cities and towns of Israel, and later when in the spring of 1987 we undertook a prayer journey to seven European capitals, we formulated a strategy which we used in our intercession for the cities. I have chosen this second journey to tell you about in some detail, to illustrate the strategy that we used. We went to Brussels, Paris, Bonn, Rome, Athens, Budapest and Warsaw.

Proclaiming Jesus as King

We began by proclaiming the Lordship of Jesus. We proclaim a victory that has already been won. *"We will shout for joy when you are victorious and will lift up our banners in the name of our God."*

(Ps. 20: 5)

The Father has himself installed his Son as king, and has given the Son the ends of the earth for his possession as a coronation present. (Ps. 2) There is a rebellion in progress against the throne, but God laughs when he sees it. Seen from the throne, the whole rebellion against Christ is no more than a ripple on the water surface from a raindrop. *"Surely the nations are like a drop in a bucket; they are regarded as dust on the scales; he weighs the islands as though they were fine dust."*

(Is. 40:15)

When we look outward from the point of view of the throne, everything assumes its proper proportion. Jesus has been crowned with glory and honour in heaven. We give him our response from earth and proclaim him as king over Paris, Bonn, Rome or whatever city we are concerned with. It was when the Philistines heard that David had been anointed king over Israel, that they went up in full force to take David prisoner (2 Sam. 5:17). The crowning was a provocation that challenged the enemies. God had taken the initiative, and decided who should be king. All others claiming to rule over cities and nations have come too late. We are bearers of good news, proclaiming a great message: *"Your God reigns!"* (Is. 52:7) The song of praise is our way of responding to the announcement that Jesus has been crowned king of heaven and earth. We do not begin from the problem, nor from the bottom. We begin by fixing our attention on the throne and we then proceed from the top, the position of victory, to the bottom, dealing with the problem itself.

Coming into harmony with the Lord and with each other

When we come before the throne, we come into God's holy presence, and so have to humble ourselves before him. We confess any obstacle in our life that the Holy Spirit may put his finger on. At every place we visited on our journey, we experienced the searching of the Spirit. At one stage, the searching was on the personal level. At the next stage, we stood in the gap in defence of the people. We stood between the Lord and the people, just as Moses did. We did not set up any system, but I discovered something remarkable. When, later, we came to the stage when we were ready for prayer war, the confession by God's people had led the way to the actual place where the prayer war should be conducted. In Paris we were led, amongst other things, to wage spiritual war against the spirit of revolution, which was released over the world through the French Revolution. We held our prayer conference a few blocks away from the Bastille, where the revolution began. We established that many of the world's revolutions could be traced back to Paris and to France, even Khomeini and the Islamic revolution.

When God's Spirit began to work in the prayer conference in Paris, people started to confess about grumbles and complaints in the church. "Lord, I confess that I have lived with a judging attitude towards the church leaders", prayed one person. "Give me a new heart in my relationship with my wife." "Forgive me for my irritation with the police; I now want to pray for the governing authorities, and I confess that there is pride in me." "Lord, I confess that I have confrontation and conflict within me when I meet brothers or sisters. Give me a natural relationship with my brothers and sisters." When God's people stood in the gap, they confessed the independence and pride that characterises many Frenchmen. It varied from town to town, and I learnt that in preparing for the spiritual battle, God's people have to humble themselves before the mighty hand of God. When we have humbled ourselves, then we have confidence to go in and do battle against evil. Judgement begins at the house of God. After that, God can deal with the world. (1 Pet. 4: 17–18) Healing happens when God's people humble themselves before God. (2 Chron. 7:14)

Unity as the foundation for agreeing in prayer

It is the task of the church to bind and to loose, in relation to powers that rule over cities and nations. We can carry out this task as long as we are assembled under the lordship of Jesus and are brought together in unity in Christ. (Matt. 18:18–19)

When we reach true agreement in prayer together, it arises from the unity that God has created between us. We took time to allow the body to come into harmony, so that we could go forward as a people brought together in the presence of God. God's Spirit brought unity between those who were present. Evangelists and pastors were reconciled to one another. In Paris, the leaders of Intercessors for France came forward and asked their fellow intercessors to forgive them for promising to do things and not carrying them out. In Belgium there was reconciliation between Catholics and Protestants, between French and Flemish speaking people, between Belgians and Germans. French people confessed that they had told disparaging jokes about Belgians. Belgians confessed wrong attitudes to Jews, and Jews who were present gave them their forgiveness in Jesus' name.

All these things happened on the personal level, but we also reached a stage when people came forward as representatives of their groups. A Pentecostalist asked forgiveness for his attitude in opposing the charismatics. Some charismatics confessed their wrong attitude towards the Pentecostalists. In some cases we had found out in advance the nature of the divisions that existed between God's people and in the nation. The Lord saw to it that we always had representatives present to stand for the groups that needed to be reconciled.

In France there were Catholics who confessed concerning the massacres, when 15,000 Protestants had been drowned in the river Seine and when the Huguenots had been driven out of France. There was present with us a Danish descendant of Huguenot exiles, who was able to represent the Huguenots in the act of reconciliation, and there was also present a descendant of a Protestant family that had suffered in the massacre. They had the date of the massacre written on their house, where many generations of the family had lived, and where there had always been a tradition of fostering bitterness and hate against Catholics from early childhood.

In Hungary, the Catholic Church had persecuted Reformed pastors. Two centuries earlier, forty Reformed pastors were condemned to be galley-slaves, and they died or disappeared in prison and never came back. A Catholic leader asked forgiveness for this action, and some Reformed pastors came forward and asked forgiveness for their attitude towards Catholics. They confessed that their hearts were so hard that if they had had the political power to do so, they would have acted in exactly the same manner towards the Catholics. All these confessions melted our hearts, there were tears in our eyes and we often heard the sound of loud weeping.

In Rome, several people confessed that they were defeated and depressed. We did not come into harmony in the body of Christ, until we had met together and prayed personally for each one of those who were confessing, ministering to them for encouragement in the power of the Holy Spirit and freeing them from depression, disappointment and their mood of defeat.

Blessing God's people, the city and the authorities

Before we can enter into prayer battle and pray *against* the powers of darkness, we must pray *for* people. We do not want to be known as people who are always praying against things.

"I urge, then, first of all, that requests, prayers, intercession and thanksgiving be made for everyone – for kings and all those in authority, that we may live peaceful and quiet lives in all godliness and holiness."

(1 Tim. 2:1–2)

We are not making war against people. We thank God for people and bless them. By prayer we can pour out love over mankind. So we blessed the various churches and denominations. We blessed the people of the city. We thanked God for each president, royal family, prime minister and government.

"For God so loved the world that he gave his only begotten Son".

(John 3:16)

We prayed for the world in the outpoured love of God. Sometimes we focused on special groups whom we are particularly wished to bless, such as families, the younger generation, immigrant groups, or the Jewish community.

Praying in a positive way is an area in which we need to discipline ourselves. As intercessors, we are called to support evangelists and evangelism in prayer. It has become part of our prayer discipline to ask: What are the churches doing in the near future to reach out in evangelism? Is there any evangelist being invited to come to your town? We come, as intercessors, to prepare the way for evangelism. If we have done our job well, the fruit will be a

58

greater freedom to evangelise, more people coming to the Lord, and growing churches. We have learnt that the best timing for a prayer offensive is just before an evangelistic campaign starts.

Prayer war

In sharing with you our strategy from our intercession for the European capitals, I should make it clear that I am describing three-day prayer conferences. By the step-by-step strategy that we used, we built up, in pursuance of our purpose, a state of readiness for battle as the army of the Lamb. Our task is to prepare God's people to come together in the Spirit. Our battle is against the spirit principalities, and through spiritual discernment we seek the Lord for light and revelation as to who the chief enemy may be. Jesus asked the demon-possessed man who lived among the tombs: *"What is your name?" "Legion", he replied, because many demons had gone into him.*

(Luke 8:30)

A legion is a whole army unit, an entire network of demonic forces. Our task is to find out who is the chief enemy and to bind the strong man.

> *"Or again, how can anyone enter a strong man's house and carry off his possessions unless he first ties up the strong man? Then he can rob his house."*
>
> (Matt. 12:29)

The process of defining what powers ruled over the city, began often when we met with the leaders of Christian churches and groups. Such maturity and spiritual discernment exists these days among God's people. Sometimes there was such unanimity between the leaders that we had no need to hesitate. We could define perhaps four or five main areas for prayer war. In some towns we met people with a special calling to investigate and obtain material for prayer war. In Germany there is Siegfried Fritsch, who has written a book of over 500 pages about the spirit over Germany, in which he looks for the roots in the pagan world-view of the Germans, in the occult, in the history of Germany through the ages right up to the Third Reich, in the relationship between Israel and Germany and the spiritual significance of the national anthem, in liberal theology, and so on. When Intercessors for Germany hold a conference in any town, Siegfried Fritsch carries out a thorough research beforehand into the history of that town, giving material for intercession. In Brussels, Paris, Bonn and Budapest there was preparation material of this kind for our prayer warfare.

Our prayer journey confirmed that individuals exist today with a gift for prophetic espionage. Certain people who have experience of God's holiness and his steadfast love, while in worship before him, have been given a hunting instinct to track down the enemy's manipulations. Evil is something that we can localise and give a name to, by studying history, observing public opinions and trends, tracing the hiding-places and headquarters of the occult, and exposing all forms of evil whether from the past or present, open or secret. This sort of investigation becomes a confirmation of God's direct prophetic word.

In Brussels we spent the entire conference period in this process of quietly seeking the Lord to find out what powers were ruling over Brussels. Those present wrote down Bible verses, visions or "pictures", and words of prophecy. When we put all this information together, we got a clear picture of the two main enemies we had to fight against: Mammon and the Harlot, materialism and immorality. It "happened" that for each prayer area we were going to deal with in prayer war, we had seven testimonies and confirmations that all accorded with one another.

Preparation for prayer war

We taught about prayer war, and gave instructions on how we would proceed so as to be able to work in unity together. Often we chose a few people to come forward and pray on behalf of everyone. At one stage we would all speak in tongues together. At another time, the one leading prayer would formulate a prayer and the whole group would repeat it in unison sentence by sentence. We taught about what we can do according to God's word. We can carry into effect the victory of Jesus, won on the Cross. He disarmed the principalities and powers of the spirit world. He made a public spectacle of them (Col. 2:15) putting them to shame. He exposed and unmasked them. From various scriptures we derive

61

the authority to act, to bind the spiritual powers, to disarm them, expose them, bring their plans to nothing, destroy their network, and break down their strongholds. So we took pains to make the intercessors fully informed, so that we could all agree together. Sometimes we found it necessary to give thorough information at one meeting, giving people time to think through the information, and then at the following meeting we could go into action in prayer war. In Budapest we had to wait for two whole days until we heard the tone of boldness in the pastors' prayers. Only then were we ready to go into prayer battle.

Praying for protection

We have learnt that before we start the prayer battle, we should pray for protection. We need the shield of faith, with which we can extinguish all the flaming arrows of the evil one. We pray for our families at home, for our possessions, for the weakest. We know our enemy is evil and cunning and that he attacks the weak, the lonely, the unprepared. We proclaim that in God's kingdom there is a rule that those who stay at home with the supplies are to share equally in the victory and the spoils with those in the firing line. (1 Sam. 30:24–25) Those who back us up by staying with the baggage are to share the benefit of what we give out in our prayer war. We do it for their sakes, and we make them participators in our victory.

Following a strategy

Prayer battles must be waged with strategy. Jesus Christ, the leader of our army, is a strategist. For our prayer journey to seven European capitals, Rolland Smith, a leader in our team, had received clear instructions. He was to call together a group in each city to represent the body of Christ. They should be people with a calling for their city and for their nation. He should therefore take with him an international team of leaders. Further, it should be an international prayer team. It was clear that all these instructions were strategic. In several places we came to realise that the enemy was working far beyond the city, on an international level. We were dealing with a world ruler. For example, there were the Greek gods and their influence over men's thinking, through Greek philosophy. We were a group from about twenty different countries, yet when it came to dealing with the Greek gods, all testified that the influence of these gods over men's minds was a problem in their lands. When we deal with international problems, we need to be an international house of prayer, exactly as Jesus said, "My house will be called a house of prayer for all nations." If Rolland Smith had not had a sensitive ear for these instructions about strategy at all stages, we would not have been able to achieve victory in the various cities. We visited the headquarters of the European Community in Brussels and met the international prayer group who pray there. When the Lord sent us to pray about international problems, he wanted the prayer group to be strategically composed, and therefore international.

Prophetic prayer war

When a spiritual battle is to take place, the timing and the location are important. We experienced time after time that the Holy Spirit led us at the right time to the right place to pray. In the Old Testament, we read of prophets giving instructions about strategy. Who is to be chosen to take part in the battle? Who will begin the battle? What weapons shall we use this time? What instructions should be given about our fighting spirit?

In Bonn I exhorted all the 320 intercessors to have that same fighting spirit that Phinehas the priest had, he who was zealous with the zeal of God. (Num. 25: 6–13) God is a consuming fire; he is jealous in his love, and he wants to have his own people for himself. It was to be a spirit of zeal just as God's zeal was, like that of Phinehas, for God's honour, because we were dealing with spiritual immorality. There were a number of examples of how liberal theology had opened the door to the occult, leading ultimately to sexual magic. We had to deal with a spiritual power of immorality of the same kind as the one that led the children of Israel astray at Baal-Peor.

In Paris, the fighting spirit was of quite a different kind. The keyword, which our French brother Philippe Dupont received and passed on to us, was humility. Jesus came, poor, riding on a donkey, meek and humble, yet the Word says that he was victorious when he rode into Jerusalem.

What judgment are we to pronounce over the evil powers? The saints are going to judge the world and the angels. An ordinary civil judge states what the law is when he pronounces judgement. We quote from the Bible when we judge the spiritual princes ruling cities and nations. We are to pronounce over them the judgement written in the Word. (Ps. 149:8–9) When we have defined who the enemy is, then we also find in God's word, under the Spirit's direction, the appropriate judgement to be pronounced over him. Prayer is a weapon of precision.

Finding the strategy from God's word

Many battles are described in the Bible. True, the battle we are waging today is on the spiritual plane, but the enemies are the same. The powers that lay behind the empires of Babylon, of Assyria, and of Greece – those powers are the same personalities today. They are depicted in the Bible as wild beasts, and such wild beasts still exist today. The demonic powers that ruled among the tribes of Canaan remained with them in their migrations, when the tribes who were associated with them were scattered among other peoples. Therefore, they are spread all over the world today. These demonic powers have not changed; they have been present for several thousand years. The good angels are also still with us, never ageing. The same heavenly armies of angels who support us today were there at the fall of Jericho, and marched in the tops of the trees in the time of David. We have been deceived into thinking that the world of the Old Testament is out-of-date. The evil powers described in it are the same evil powers that we have to deal with today, and these powers are not creative. Their only creative characteristic is their ability to change their disguise and appear under new names and in new shapes, but they remain the same old crew as before. The old Greek gods are worshipped today on the ancient places of sacrifice, though now in the form of saints in the Greek Orthodox church. In Scandinavia the Greek gods have acquired Old Norse names and are called "asa-gods". In fact they are the same old demonic powers that opposed God's people in the Old Testament. That is why the descriptions of battles in the Old Testament are so relevant today. But in those days the evil spirits could not be driven out in the name of Jesus; that is the difference. We fight in the strength of the victory of Jesus.

When I am preparing for prayer war, I try with the help of the Spirit to find, among the various confrontations in the Bible, the one that most resembles the situation I am now facing.

Bonn, Germany

In Bonn we fought our battle in accordance with Joshua 10:1–25. I received this before coming to Bonn. The Lord spoke to my heart and said, "Follow the strategy that Joshua used in his battle against the five kings at Gibeon." I saw that Joshua made a lightning attack after an all-night march. I asked the international prayer team to hold a prayer watch for the 24 hours immediately before the conference began. They took turns in praying through the night. It was our own way of marching all night and then making a sudden attack. Then, together with the German team, we were able to define the enemies in the spiritual battle, and to distinguish five principal spirits:

1. *A spirit of spiritual immorality.*
2. *A religious spirit, leading Christians to live in unreality, a spirit of outward show.*
3. *A spirit of death, acting both through abortions and through childlessness.*
4. *Humanism and materialism.*
5. *A spirit of fatherlessness.*

Joshua fought against five kings, who had entered into alliance with one another. He did not intervene until the people of Gibeon asked for his help. We waited until the German leaders' team expressed their willingness to have our help in the spiritual battle, and that gave us the freedom to intervene.

Rome and Athens

In Rome we were able to define one of the opposing powers as a spirit of conspiracy at work in the highest places. We took our strategy from the way in which Absalom's conspiracy against David was suppressed.
· In Athens our strategy was made clear from Zec. 9:13–17; 10:1–5, which fitted perfectly with Greece.

Unity is given to intercessors when they direct their thoughts to God's Word. God's Spirit then brings the Word to life for them so that they are motivated to carry through the agreed strategy.

So these are just a few examples of how it is possible to enter into the spirit of a battle from the Bible in prayer for a city today. Almost always when I am leading prayer war, the Lord gives me a chapter that helps me to define the battlefield, and to find the strategy to suit the situation I am facing.

Performing prophetic acts

One aspect of prayer war is the carrying out of prophetic acts. We were to do this in each of the seven capital cities. In Hungary, we realised that we were fighting against a spirit of slavery, a power like that found in the Assyrian empire. When freedom was proclaimed in the land, both Nehemiah and Jeremiah had to see to it that the prisoners were indeed set free. Nehemiah did a prophetic act before the people. He urged the leaders to free their brothers, and then he shook out the folds of his robe and said, *"In this way may God shake out of his house and possessions every man who does not keep this promise. So may such a man be shaken out and emptied!" At this the whole assembly said, "Amen", and praised the Lord.*

(Neh. 5:13)

When we came against the spirit of slavery and proclaimed freedom in Budapest, we all stood and shook our jackets and clothes as a prophetic act. May the Lord shake up those who do not release their brothers, just as we are shaking our jackets! We shook them violently under the power of the Holy Spirit.

In Warsaw we were to carry out prophetic, symbolic acts as we welcomed the Lord as judge over the people. We did what Joshua did in front of Mount Ebal and Mount Gerizim according to Jos. 8:33–35, reading out all the blessings and the curses written in Deut. 27 and 28. The man who stood in front of the tall pillar in the hall where we met, and read out the blessings, was a Jew of the tribe of Issachar, in accordance with Moses' instructions in Deut. 27:12. When we perform prophetic acts, the Holy Spirit often helps us with the details. There are many prophetic acts described in Scripture, and the Holy Spirit brings them to life for us, like the producer of a play directing the actors.

Under the inspiration of the Holy Spirit, we did acts that the prophets had done. We did things in the spirit, in the unseen, which will later come to be revealed and visible.

Proclaiming the victory and releasing the Lord's anointing

When we have driven out the evil spirits, we are not to leave the house empty. We are to fill up the empty space left by the departure of the enemies. After we have carried out prayer warfare, therefore, the normal thing is to pray for an outpouring of the Holy

Spirit. The reign of evil spirits needs to be replaced by the reign of the saints. After we have done warfare against the strong man, we pray for strong Christian leadership to be raised up to replace the enemy. After we have destroyed and overthrown the enemy positions, there comes a time to build and to plant. (Jer. 1:10)

The last meeting in every prayer conference was announced as a proclamation meeting. What had been prayer burdens when we began, became faith proclamations when we ended. When the breakthrough has come after a long battle and you know that the Lord has answered your prayer, you are ready to proclaim a new beginning.

Rolland Smith described, in the following way, the strategy which we followed leading up to the final proclamation meeting in each of the places we visited:

"The strategy behind Operation Europe is this: We are mobilising God's army for battle. We are uniting with the Lord and with the angels of heaven in a co-ordinated attack against the spiritual powers that hold the nations imprisoned. Then with the authority of a unanimous agreement in the Lord (Matt. 18:18–20), we shall release God's blessing over Europe. The Lord has promised us that the long-awaited release of evangelistic anointing in accordance with Isaiah 61 is coming with a mighty outpouring of God's Spirit and with a great harvest of souls for God's kingdom. God is now releasing people, resources, power and wisdom in order to take whole cities for God's kingdom. We now proclaim that it is God's time for Europe. We call upon the wind of the Spirit to blow from the four corners of the earth. Now we shall not be hearing only of awakening at the ends of the earth. Now is God's time for Europe. The Spirit and the anointing that were over Jesus when he was sent to announce the message of good news for the poor and release for the prisoners, that same anointing we now release over the Body of Christ."

It was not only Rolland Smith who released blessings and proclaimed victory for Europe, but also the others in the team, and the leaders and intercessors in the cities we visited. We spoke a special language in the meetings. Often we read some powerful scripture and trumpeted it out together like heralds. "We proclaim that the time has now come when this word will be fulfilled in Rome", in Paris, and so on.

Releasing a spirit of grace and prayer over Germany

I want you to get the feeling of how we spoke in these proclamation meetings. Openness arose out of the unity that we experienced with God's people, and our openness in prayer together. Each of the team spoke from the background of his own calling, the field that lay nearest to him. We had, also, many words from praying folk and leaders who joined in battle with us and wished too to be associated with us in proclaiming the victory. We often began a proclamation meeting by proclaiming Jesus as king and Lord. This is the wording of my proclamation in Bonn:

"The Lord has promised that he will pour out a

spirit of grace and supplication. (Zec. 12:10) That spirit of prayer, which has already come upon groups of Messianic Jews in Israel, I now release over God's people in Germany. A spirit of prayer was poured out on David's house. That means that the spirit of prayer that is now being poured out on you will enable you to rule like David's house, with Christ. A spirit of prayer was also poured out on the inhabitants of Jerusalem. That means a spirit of prayer over Germany leading to prayer altars being raised up in the cities and towns, where Christians can come together in unity and pray for their city. A spirit of prayer was poured out on families. That means that the time has now come when it will be easier for father and mother to gather their family to pray, and to call on all their relatives to seek after God. The Lord roars like a lion. Why are you roaring like a lion, Lord? My Spirit roars for the anointing of Elijah, that it may be poured out on men and women in the end-time. The time has now come for you to pray in the spirit and power of Elijah, and to come together to prepare the way for the return of Jesus. Now you will share in the anointing that was upon Jehu. He was anointed as king by Elijah to root out idol-worship from Israel. The time has now come when the Lord is anointing his servants to root out occultism and superstition, to work together with the stormy wind of the Lord. Sound the alarm on my holy mountain! Blow the trumpet! You are called to mobilise the army of the Lamb for battle in the day of the Lord. Call up the prayer warriors! Raise up your young men from 25 to 40 years old. The Lord gives you a commission as he gave one to Joshua. You are to be an officer in the Lord's army! The Lord is going to train you to lead great prayer meetings. You will be leading 500 people, yes, even 5000 in time to come. No, that is not enough, you will be capable of leading meetings where ten thousand come together to pray. Raise up prayer altars in your towns; you are to start a prayer mountain where people will gather to pray day and night. I proclaim that the time has now come for you to take your places and reign with Jesus."

The leader of Intercessors for Germany, Berthold Becker, says that our days of prayer in Bonn were a breakthrough for the prayer movement in Germany. The number of intercessors has increased, and prayer altars have been raised up in the cities by intercessors who meet regularly to pray for their city. The prayer movement in Germany is among the strongest and best in Europe.

Relations with Israel and the Jews

We had a Jewish believer with us in our team of leaders, Steve Lightle. He acted as an ambassador for the Jewish people. God has never broken his agreement with Abraham. He has promised blessing upon the seed of Abraham, and through Abraham all the families of the earth are to be blessed. He who blesses Abraham, God has promised to bless. He who curses Abraham, God will curse. God has promised that all Israel will be saved, and their restoration will bring riches for all the world. We pray that the veil will be taken away from their minds and they will recognise their Messiah; and that the Spirit will be poured out on them.

In order for a city or a nation to conform with the kingdom of God, to come into harmony with the coming Messianic kingdom, we need to watch the relationship between that city or nation, and Israel. On our journey, we dealt with anti-semitism everywhere. Jews had been exposed to anti-semitic acts in Belgium, Germany and France. While political slogans were being scrawled on walls and fences in France, swastikas and anti-semitic slogans were being scrawled in Rome. Greece surrendered Jews to Hitler's gas chambers, and was the country that we found the most unaware, in Europe, of Israel's role in the prophetic scheme of events. Yet everywhere we found intercessors who were willing to stand in the gap for the responsibility of their people to pray for forgiveness for, and cleansing from, anti-semitism. We sought to make God's people ready to serve the Jews when they would be coming out from the Soviet Union and from all other nations where they still were, and are.

Jews who believe in the Messiah

Everywhere we went, we saw evidence that the Lord was at work among Jewish people. In Paris, an international musician, who was a Jew, came and listened to Steve Lightle. It was the first time he had been in a church and heard a Jew who could explain his faith in Jesus as Messiah. He received Jesus as his own

Messiah. In Rome, a young Israeli, who was studying to become a doctor, was baptised in the Holy Spirit. An elderly Jewish man, who came in from the street, was so impressed by the power that he saw in Steve Lightle, that he came up during the after-meeting and said, "I want to have the power that you have." Steve Lightle was able to show him how he could receive Jesus as Messiah. We had local Jewish believers with us in every prayer conference. Today there are true, living churches where the wall of division between Jew and Gentile has been broken down, and where the two peoples can meet and worship the Lord together.

If you seek the best for your area, and a place for it in God's kingdom, you need to be sure of its proper relationship with what God is doing in restoring the Jewish people. We ourselves could not go in and release God's blessings in a place without first showing to the people how Israel fits into the picture.

Answers to prayer

The vision behind the prayer journey was to send a spiritual commando unit through Europe in order to break the powers of darkness, that have hindered a breakthrough for the Gospel in our day on this ancient Christian territory. We wanted to defend the end-time harvest field, believing in a great ingathering of souls. The Lord has answered our prayers. Today, Europe is wide open to the Gospel. There are no more closed doors or frontiers. Even Albania has opened its borders. Persecution has ended, and

Christians are no longer in communist prisons. There is freedom to hold evangelistic campaigns in the former communist countries.

When we were in Budapest, we identified the strong man over Hungary as a spirit of slavery, which had left both the Church and the people in a state of hopelessness. I remember that there were 15 pastors and leaders in agreement with us to cast out the spirit of slavery and proclaim freedom for Hungary. The answer to our prayer came when, two years later, the barbed wire around the borders was cut down and sold as souvenirs, and Hungarians could travel freely to other countries once more. Since our prayer journey I have met, in Germany and Israel, some of the Hungarian pastors who prayed against that spirit of slavery, and they say, "Now we have freedom, we hold international passports and are allowed to travel to other countries. This is a fruit of the victory over the strong man of slavery."

Our prayer team was in Paris on the 1st May, and we were able to come against the world-wide spirit of revolution. We wanted to get at the root of the May Day demonstrations in the socialist countries. So, we prayed in the Place de la Bastille in Paris, where a statue of a woman stands, called "The Spirit of Revolution". Since we prayed there, the May Day celebrations in the former communist and socialist countries have lost their power to attract the crowds. May Day in these countries used to be a public holiday with no room for the Lord, when Christians who met to worship Jesus were suspected by others

76

of not being loyal to their country. Today, this yoke has been broken.

Chapter 6

Invasion

We generally consider prayer war in three stages:

1. **Research**. Do all you can to gather information, to make yourself well-informed.
2. **Strategy**. Seek the Lord for his strategy.
3. **Attack**. When you have done all the preparation and know that God's appointed time has come, then you can give the order for prayer invasion.

It may be that you decide to have a period of concentrated prayer for a place, but when I use the expression "prayer invasion", I mean going to places to pray on the spot. There was a time when all the prayer gatherings I attended were held in a church hall or in a prayer group meeting in a home. Now, however, we end up praying in the streets, in the town square, in the shopping centres, outside town hall, or in the gates of the city. We find that we need to seek out the places where people actually are, who are there to be won for the Lord. These are the places where, at the next stage, the evangelists will be reaching out to win souls.

Philip invades the capital of Samaria

The way in which Philip invaded the capital city of Samaria (Acts 8) to establish God's kingdom there, is equally applicable today. It was a successful invasion, because there was great joy in the city. Our aim in conquering is that there will be great joy, great peace, much righteousness, and a flooding of heavenly atmosphere by the outpouring of the Holy Spirit. That is what happens when the kingdom of God comes into a place.

Freeing of individuals

Philip proclaimed Christ. One by one, individuals were delivered and healed in Jesus' name.

> *"With shrieks, evil spirits came out of many, and many paralytics and cripples were healed."*
>
> (Acts 8: 7)

Freeing a town means, first, freeing individuals. An evangelist in Italy, who was building up a Catholic charismatic community, told how, out of those who were saved, 70 percent needed to be delivered from evil spirits. An equal percentage had been involved in the occult. Pastors in Sikkim, in northern India, told how every single person who became a member of their churches needed to be delivered from evil spirits when they came to the Lord.

Breaking the demonic network

In Samaria there was an occult network. Simon the sorcerer had struck the people with amazement, and all the people, both high and low, gave him their attention. The sorcerer had power to bind people to himself; in fact, his power was so great that all the people were bound to him. On one occasion in Pakistan, I saw about fifty people all delivered from evil spirits at the same time. It appeared that most of them had been to worship at the grave of a holy man. The fakir who looked after the shrine had a power of binding people to himself by demonic forces so that they had to return periodically to the grave. Our task was to break up a whole demonic network in that part of Lahore. Part of the freeing of a place consists in destroying demonic networks that binds groups of people to one another.

Holding the ground by stopping infiltration

The only thing that could have prevented a total victory in Samaria would have been the enemy infiltrating the church. Therefore, the enemy's tactic was to get Simon the sorcerer present at the laying on of hands in the church, when the Holy Spirit was given to the expectant people. It is one of his cleverest ways of sowing weeds among the wheat. The sorcerer wanted to take part, and to lay unclean hands on people. He offered money so that he might have the same power as the apostles, but they exposed his wickedness, so the enemy's plan to contaminate the church by infiltration was thwarted. But the enemy has succeeded with this tactic in many churches. A church that has been infiltrated and contaminated cannot be God's instrument for taking the city. What happens is that the kingdom of darkness captures the church, instead of the church taking the city for Christ.

I believe in Philip's strategy in his invasion of the capital of Samaria. He not only succeeded in taking the city, but he and the apostles also had the wisdom to hold the captured ground.

Establishing free zones

To take a city is to establish a free territory. This is done first and foremost on the personal level. The place where you live can be a liberated area, a free zone where the kingdom of light prevails. When Jesus taught about the light, he said that the whole body can have light.

> *"See to it, then, that the light within you is not darkness. Therefore, if your whole body is full of light, and no part of it dark, it will be completely lighted, as when the light of a lamp shines on you."*
>
> (Luke 11:35–36)

You can be so governed by the light that Jesus brings with him, that no part of you is dark. When I read this scripture many years ago, I realised that I had an area in my life that was covered in darkness. I had a habit of teasing people, in a way that caused hurt to them, when I was feeling cheerful. I teased my wife Lena about certain unusual dialect words that she used, and hurt her to tears many times. I did not want to do it, and I used to ask both her and God for forgiveness. "You are so like your grand-father", said my close relatives. He used to tease my grandmother, when he was in a good mood, and as a child, sitting in the back seat of their car, I used to hear him doing this. There came a point when I asked for help in being set free from this area of darkness and family curse in my life. Jesus released me and gave me light. The area of your life should be a free zone full of light. When many such personal free zones are created in a place, the light in the place becomes brighter. The children of Israel had light in the places where they lived, while total dark-ness covered all Egypt for three days. Your home should be a free zone of light; in this way the place where you live will be conquered for Christ.

But the Bible speaks also of free cities, to which a person could flee to seek refuge from the avenger of blood. Christ is the fulfilment of the vision con-cerning the city of refuge. We take our refuge in him. But God, who gave the instructions for six cities of refuge to be reserved in Israel, is concerned for the establishing of cities of refuge in the end-time, free cities where people can escape from darkness and from the avenger of blood. Is the place where you live going to be a liberated area, a free city?

"Explosion", Canberra

The Lord's storm-troops are to storm the cities and invade the streets.

> *They rush upon the city; they run along the wall. They climb into the houses, . . . The Lord thunders at the head of his army; his forces are beyond number, and mighty are those who obey his command.*
>
> (Joel 2:9, 11)

The spiritual storm-troops have a first division, the intercessors, who go forward and clear the way in the spirit. Then comes the second division, consisting of evangelists, who storm in, invading the city with the good news that Jesus saves, heals the sick and sets people free. To help you to begin thinking and planning for the spiritual invasion of an area, I will give you, as an example, some of the preparation we did for an invasion of the Australian capital, Canberra, in August 1987. International Outreach mobilised 500 Christians to invade Canberra and storm its streets with the gospel. About twenty churches united in a month's campaign, culminating in the hiring of the city's biggest indoor arena, holding 5,000 people. The 500 Christians from other countries joined with the members of the local churches to train as spiritual warriors, and were then sent out into streets, squares, houses and homes for two weeks of guerrilla prayer war. Stuart Gramenz, who was leading the campaign, had used this method during campaigns in India, where teams went out on the streets and into the market-places and prayed for the sick, who were healed from leprosy, blindness, deafness and dumbness. The lame began to walk, and the blind received their sight.

Training-camps for soldiers

A soldier sent into battle unable to handle his rifle or his hand-grenades would be almost helpless. He would be constantly frightened, with no way of defending himself, and in the end he himself would most likely be shot.

Some Christians get shot to pieces when it comes to witnessing and praying for the sick. Others are conscious of God's power, but believe that the gift of praying for the sick is given to a few specially chosen people, while the rest look on.

The basic weapons for every private in God's army are sharing the gospel, laying hands on the sick, and casting out demons. These are your rifle and your grenades. Without them you will experience fear and defeat. Equipped with them, you will know a new boldness and power in your life.

"We want to initiate a spiritual explosion of the power of God among the population of Canberra, through those whom we shall be training, and we intend to give them ammunition to defend themselves, those whom they love, and others", said the leaders of International Outreach. The 500 from other countries and the infantry from the local churches were trained by means of three workshop courses, as follows:

1. How you can become as bold as a lion.
This workshop was suitable for those who needed boldness in all areas of their lives, but particularly for those who felt inadequate when it came to sharing their faith with others.

2. How the sick are healed.
God's healing power can be released through every Christian. In this workshop, there was clear teaching on the foundations of praying for the sick.

3. How to become one of God's guerrillas.
The centre of gravity of the programme for the "healing explosion" was to equip the saints and then to send them out to bear witness of Jesus' power to save and to heal. They were not to wait for an evangelist coming in from somewhere else, to pray for the sick. They were to invite people to the meetings by offering to pray for them. They were to be equipped to lay hands on people on streets and in squares, and these actions would result from their training in prayer war.

The prayer invasion of Canberra

Intercessors for Australia had been invited to share in the prayer preparation for the evangelistic campaign in Canberra. First we met with a group of pastors. I spoke to them about their responsibility as elders in the city. I also put before them the plans we had for prayer war. Since we came from other countries, we needed to submit ourselves to the spiritual leaders on the ground and to seek their blessing for the mission. We received their blessing and their prayers for us, and they laid hands on us and prophesied over us in a way that gave us instructions for what followed.

The intercessors met together over a five-day period. To help with the prayer strategy, one person had helped us with research into the occult organisations so that they could all be marked on a map of Canberra. So we knew where the Masons had their HQ, where the Spiritist meetings, Yoga centres, witches' covens, Hare Krishna, and so on, were all situated. Altogether there were 74 different groups marked on the map. One prayer group of Christian university students had great experience of prayer war, and they were able to give us supplementary information on the structure of the kingdom of darkness in Canberra. We were told where the aboriginal people's old sacrificial high places were, and how these ritual places were used today by Satan-worshippers and New Age people. We were told of a park where crucified kangaroos had been found. All this information was of use later when we gathered for prayer war.

The map markings came as a surprise to the pastors, but also explained to them why it had always been particularly hard to get church members in certain residential areas. Wherever there was an accumulation of occult movements, there was a dearth of active Christians. One pastor had been very surprised that he had so few members who lived immediately around his church. Around his church were three yoga centres. One Thursday evening we prayed that if there were any other hidden occult centre near the church, it would be exposed and spiritually disarmed. In the Sunday newspaper three days later there was an article exposing the existence of a witches' coven meeting very near the church where our prayer meetings were taking place.

Training camp for prayer battle

At the headquarters base of Youth with a Mission in Canberra, we held a course of seven days' training for prayer war. The 160 people taking part in it came from all the states of Australia. There were about a hundred men, mostly young. The purpose was to train them to be officers in the Lord's army. I gave teaching on the army of the Lamb, on fighting spirit, on the task of prayer, taking a city, how to identify the spiritual enemies, the need to break down the high places of sacrifice and the altars to strange gods, strategy and courses of action in prayer battle, and how the Holy Spirit gives detailed battle instructions. It was the first time that the Intercessors for Australia had held a prayer conference comprising more men than women.

Reconciliation between aboriginals and whites

We saw, as we came together, a process of deep reconciliation between Australian aboriginals and whites. We had a group of aboriginals among us. One white man stood up and asked them for forgiveness for the hatred in his heart; his wife had been the victim of an attempted rape by an aboriginal. A Pentecostal pastor asked forgiveness for his ancestor, who had been a member of a hunting party exterminating all the aboriginals from the island of Tasmania. Several of the young men had taken part in fights between aboriginals and whites, and asked forgiveness. There were women who had married into families with colour prejudice. There were Chinese people, who confessed that they had pride in their hearts when they compared themselves with aboriginals. I believe there were about fifty of the 160 people taking part, who broke down and asked the aboriginal people to forgive them. The same process of reconciliation also took place between Catholics and Protestants. The walls of division were broken down at the cross of Jesus. There was a welding together into unity among the whole group, and a releasing of joy, songs of praise and fighting spirit.

Co-ordination in the two opposing kingdoms

Our aboriginal brothers truly understood prayer war. Their knowledge was badly needed, as many of the New Age movements are connected to the old pagan religion and practice. On 17th August 1987, the New Age people had gathered at twenty of the sacred sites, the high places of sacrifice that they recognised as the dwelling-places of gods and spirits. In meditation, they made contact with the spirits in order to connect together their world-wide spiritual network, and they co-ordinated their action with the aboriginals. Even in Sweden, the New Age people stood at the old sacred sites and meditated, so as to usher in the new era all over the world. I become more and more convinced that there are two kingdoms in confrontation with one another, God's kingdom and Satan's. I had prepared for our Australian visit by encouraging my friends in Sweden and other countries to stand with us in prayer. I knew that we had intercessors praying for us in all the Scandinavian countries, Israel, England, Ireland, USA, France, Germany, Nigeria, Pakistan, South Africa. We were representatives of a "house of prayer for all nations", of which Jerusalem is the centre. This was God's answer to the "harmonic convergence" which the occult movements were trying to achieve on that 17th August.

Final test: 15 simultaneous prayer offensives

As a final test at the end of a week of instruction, we sent out 15 prayer groups to invade Canberra. They were sent to the Parliament House, the Supreme Court, the National Museum of Art and the War Memorial. A group of farmers went to the Ministry of Agriculture, a group of aboriginals went to the Ministry for Aboriginal Affairs, and another group went to the University. One girl had investigated all the centres of the feminist movement, restaurants, cafes, youth hostels and witches' covens. Before they would give her the addresses, they asked her, "Are you an activist?" and she said yes, she was an activist! She was an activist for Jesus. She took a group round to all the various places and they prayed. Another group went to the different embassies. New Guinea called its Embassy a spirit house. The Indonesian Embassy had its garden full of Hindu gods, while the Thai Embassy was built like a temple, also full of idols. This group succeeded in gaining entrance to five of the embassies to pray there, and they also visited the Islamic Centre. At the Soviet Embassy they prayed for the Jews in the Soviet Union, and they went to the Israeli Embassy to bless them. An Anglican clergyman led a group who went to the headquarters of the Masons to do prayer war. Another group dealt with the three high places of sacrifice around Canberra. One group went on a mission of blessing to the sports stadium where the principal evangelistic meetings were to be held, another group went to the Jewish centre, and finally, one group went to the shopping centre. When they all returned, they were able to testify that they had been able to gain access to the places they had been sent to. The Holy Spirit had given them creative strategies, and relevant scriptures, and they had been brought, in an astonishing way, into contact with people, which opened the way for them. One elderly man had a word of knowledge about the way his group would get into the Parliament House. He knew how many stairs they had to climb, and when they had to turn to the right or left, to reach a particular room where they could pray in peace. Everything was as he had been told; they just walked in and reached their prayer room as he directed them. In previous years I had often been out on prayer offensives, but I had never before experienced 15 groups all going out at the same time in a capital city.

What was the object of this offensive? – to prepare Canberra for a time of harvest, to clear out occult influences, to storm the city so that there would be a spiritual breakthrough and so that the glory of God would fill the city, to prepare the way for Jesus.

The day after this prayer invasion, the evangelisation team of 300 people went out into the city to witness, to pray for the sick, and to expect signs and wonders to happen on the streets and in the squares. Twenty churches had co-operated in renting Bruce Stadium for holding the evangelistic meetings.

A sign of peace

After the two whole days of prayer war, we heard on the television news that there had been no murders in Australia for the past 36 hours. This was the fourth time in my experience that I had seen similar happenings, signs of the kingdom of God, in connection with prayer war. God's kingdom of peace comes when we battle against the evil spirits. Those spirits desire their regular periodic blood-sacrifices from the nations. That is why they inspire people to commit violence, murder, and abortions.

During the evangelistic campaign which followed, there were about 300 persons who made decisions to follow Christ. The team were able to pray with people on the streets, and signs and wonders took place on a greater scale than had ever before been seen in Canberra. Many who wrote from Canberra afterwards said that there was a real spiritual break-through.

In May 1988, about 35,000 to 40,000 people met to pray at the new Parliament building, which was being opened on the occasion of Australia's bicen-tennial celebrations. It was the biggest prayer meet-ing in the history of Australia. At the central prayer meeting in Canberra, Jesus was proclaimed as Lord of the nation, with the government resting upon his shoulders. A major happening at the gathering was the reconciliation, and the improvement in relations, between white and black Christians. White leaders asked the aboriginals for forgiveness for the violence that was taking place against them. The police had nothing to do during that great gathering – there was no lawlessness. An experienced journalist said that he had never seen such a large crowd behave with such obvious harmony and love.

Intercessors for Australia held a week of prayer in preparation for this great national event. The intercessors gathered in the same church building where we had met together a year earlier. Noel Bell, the leader of Intercessors for Australia, said that this was "Stage 2". He wrote: "I am sure that the prayer we had in Canberra last August laid the foundation for this second prayer week. In parentheses, the crowd of people who assembled on the following day to meet the Queen of England was between 15,000 and 20,000. We have also had reports from the opposition parties that they were strongly influenced to resist certain proposed changes to the national constitution, which would have removed all references to Christian belief. It was intended that these changes be introduced on the occasion of the bicentennial celebrations. They were opposed because 40,000 Christians had shown their care for the nation by coming to the opening of the new Parliament."

Preparing the Way

I have shown how a group of intercessors prepared the way for those who later went out to evangelise in the streets of Canberra. The small scale operation carried out by the intercessors in 1987 opened the way for the largest prayer gathering in the history of Australia in the following year. Prayer warriors are called to be pioneers, to go in on the first wave, to be front-line soldiers. A hundred years ago, when missionaries were being mobilised to go to China and other lands with the Gospel, the prayer supporters were told to stay at home and support those who went to fight in the front line. I believe we can do better than this today, and I say to the intercessors: "You go in first, and clear the way for the evangelists and those who plant new churches."

One pastor in Denmark hires a bus for a day, and fills it with praying people. Then he takes them to a place where a new church is needed, and they have a day of prayer to clear the way for it. I myself take prayer teams to hard, difficult places, closed lands, and unreached peoples.

94

A pastor in the Philippines, who has planted ten new churches in five years, says that he uses this strategy. "First, I send a group of intercessors to a place where I want to start a new church. I send them to fast and pray for two weeks, to confront the strong man, to go into his house and bind him, and when they have carried out their task, to come back and report. Then I send a team of evangelists, together with the person who is to be responsible for looking after the new church. They are sent to plunder the strong man's house and to seize his goods. That is the secret of how ten new churches were planted in five years." The Lord calls for intercessors with a pioneer spirit, who will go in first.